Mary A. Gervin—a veteran instructor and writing consultant—hails from Columbus, Georgia. After graduating from college in Atlanta, she settled in Albany, Georgia, situated along the Flint River in southwest Georgia. A graduate of Florida State University, she is a retired English professor after having spent four decades honing the skills of emerging writers and budding poets and serving as a consultant for various publishing companies and educational boards.

Mary A Gervin

FARTHER ON DOWN THE ROAD

AUSTIN MACAULEY PUBLISHERS®

LONDON • CAMBRIDGE • NEW YORK • SHARJAH

Ordering Information
Quantity sales: Special discounts are available on quantity purchases by corporations, associations, and others. For details, contact the publisher at the address below.

Publisher's Cataloging-in-Publication data
Gervin, Mary A
Farther On Down the Road

ISBN 9798891556867 (Paperback)
ISBN 9798891556874 (ePub e-book)

Library of Congress Control Number: 2024913512

www.austinmacauley.com/us

First Published 2024
Austin Macauley Publishers LLC
40 Wall Street, 33rd Floor, Suite 3302
New York, NY 10005
USA

mail-usa@austinmacauley.com
+1 (646) 5125767

Table of Contents

A Turn of Phrase

A short saying often contains much wisdom.

Confucious

A Turn of Phrase

Darkness closes in
A winter of discontent
Welcome to hard times

Finding common ground
Reaping the secret of joy
All's right with the world

One in a million
Somewhere between slim and none
Hollow victory

With Wonder

Into the unknown
Uncharted realm of suspense
Adventure awaits

Life Cycle

Birth: labor intense
Life: labor at length
Death: labor done

Ripple Effect

A rippling effect
Pot calling the kettle black
Fall wide of the mark

Finally

The final chapter
Parting is such sweet sorrow
Fun while it lasted

Sheer Genius

Take the familiar
Make it extraordinary
Creative genius

Utter Failure

Measure for measure
Falling like a lead balloon
No glimmer of hope

Procrastination

Procrastination
Walking on feet made of clay
Getting nowhere fast

Sweet Victory

Go the extra mile
In whichever way you can
Claim the victory

Devil-May-Care

Seeking destiny
Robbing Peter to pay Paul
Inherit the wind

Hope Floats

A work in progress
Domestic tranquility
Coming full circle

In Other Words

24

Flogging a dead horse
Fly by the seat of the pants
Race against the clock

In Awe

A sense of wonder
Color of the moonlit skies
Clear and natural

Stamp of Approval

Writing on the wall
All things in moderation
Seal of approval

In Limbo

27

Invisible man
A stranger in the mirror
Waiting to exhale

Designing Woman

Designing damsel
Finding the secrets of joy
Woman of substance

Unsettling

United we stand
The stark truth of the matter
Divided we fall

A Way Out

A man of means
The path of least resistance
An easy way out

Steppingstones

One step at a time
From here to eternity
Getting nowhere fast

Biding the Time

32

Once in a lifetime
Create lasting memories
Not without laughter

Entangled

Opposites attract
In league with the enemy
Taming the dragon

Need for distraction
Instant gratification
An imperfect life

Good Vibes

Streetcar named Desire
Adventures in wonderland
When love conquers all

Delight in the day
Singing through the wilderness
Admiring rainbows

Quitters never win
Slow and steady wins the race
By hook or by crook

Hidden in plain sight
Things happen for a reason
Present from the past

Life Interrupted

Poor as a pauper
Complaint to an empty purse
A bag full of dust

The woes of this world
Well-acquainted with the night
A shadow of doubt

The stuff of madness
Much ado about nothing
A sigh of relief

Great expectations
Excellence is my mantra
All for the best

Sounding Bored

Disembodied voice
Borne of a woman distressed
Battered…unbeaten…

Live in the moment
Tomorrow may be too late
Let the good times roll

Things are as they are
The best of possible worlds
Experience joy

The path to glory
All for one and one for all
A means to an end

Angst

Go the extra mile
Dance until the body breaks
The final chapter

All things in due time
The way the cookie crumbles
Broken promises

Candles in the wind
Parting in such sweet sorrow
Goodbye and good luck

Disappointment

Dashed hopes…dispersed dreams…postponed plans…
Ignored by family…friends…acquaintances…
Sick at heart…spirit of heaviness…
(At least my kitty understands my plight
Positioning herself in my lap)
Palpable pain pulsates within my soul
Ocean of tears spilled
Injured feelings…fading fervor…failed fortune…forlorn
        face…
Needing a reassuring hug…soothing smile…comforting
        word
Too little…too late
Extreme emptiness…
Downright down in the dumps.

Gumption

Master of the game
Failure is not an option
No second chances

Facing the music
Taking a bull by the horns
In the nick of time

Natural Beauty

Perfectionism
Masterpiece of creation
Grand Canyon gorge

Midsummer night's dream
Wandering through wonderland
Where nature reigns

The Breathings of My Heart

Words are the voice of the heart.

Confucius

Rest in Peace

(*In memory of our dearly departed*)

Light a candle for our expired matrons
Let it shine, flicker, show
May it reflect their time of service
Light a candle; let it glow…

Light a candle for those departed matrons
Giving brilliance for the legacy left
While the glow of their communal labors
Reflect our motto: 'He conquers who conquers himself'…

Light a candle for all our matrons
Whose behavior through the years
Reflect the ideals of Club founders
Who were stellar, steadfast, sincere…

Light a candle; let it glow
Until this earthly form we know
Surrenders, succumbing to mortality
And causes worldly toils to cease
Now somewhere over the rainbow
Our dear Club members rest in peace.

Through It All

How goes it with you this fine day?
As my reflections shifted your way
Thought I'd pen a few lines to say:
Though days and nights stretch on and on
Friends too few; you're feeling forlorn.
Though you may be a wee bit stressed
And it seems you're not at your best.
Though you consider the times as rotten,
Be of good courage; God has not forgotten.

God is faithful; He is true
Whatever the problem, whatever the news
No matter how troubling your point of view
Trust in God; He'll see you through.

Welcome Words

Pleasant words are as honeycomb
Sweet to the soul and health to the bones
Whether printed on cards or shared by phone…

It's nice to know someone helps to bear
Another's burdens, pitfalls, toils, snares
It's sweet to show that somebody cares…

In your struggle, despite sorrow or pain
At times, the journey might be strained
Be thankful; your effort is not in vain:
Trials worketh patience, an asset to attain.

Proverbially Speaking

A heart of peace gives life to the body
Good news gives health to the bones
A happy heart tames the haughty
A warm smile melts a heart of stone.

A cheerful look brings joy to the heart
A kind word helps spread cheer
A joyful heart can somehow thwart
A mournful spirit lingering near.

A wise tongue speaks timely words
To soothe, console, heal, uplift.
May you find relief or be stirred
By the sentiment of this penned script.

Hopeful

Turning over a new leaf today
Hoping the day will bring sunshine
Accepting that well-laid plans might go awry
Noting that an unwelcome surprise may be in store
Keeping a level of confidence
Feeling up to the journey ahead
Uttering a prayer of thanksgiving
Letting the Lord take control.

Idle Hours

Drawing doodles on a writing pad
Or daydreaming in front of the idiot box
Watching the performers watching me.

No chores to do nor errands to run
Time trickles timorously
Ignoring the impulse to take a nap
Mulling over random thoughts about proposed plans…
Strange people…distant vistas…
Easy breezy goes the time…

Daydreaming

Doing nothing in particular
dawdling…dabbling…doodling…
Absent-mindedly musing…mulling…commiserating…
Yielding to wishful thinking
Delving into the subliminal realm
Rambling thoughts crisscross consciousness
Ethereal visions of reality
All for nothing
Morpheus' unfocused mindlessness
Simply staring into space

Missing You

Whether in my head
       Or in my heart
Warm thoughts of you
       Remain a part
Of fond memories
Passing time at ease
Just shooting the breeze…

Hoping this brief rhyme
Finds you and your kin
Safe at this time
And at peace within.

As You Recover

Warm thoughts
Sent your way
Trusting they've wrought
A cheerful display…

As you're recovering
May God's grace
Help you in discovering
A comforting space
A bright and glorious morning
A sunny and restful afternoon
May you be blessed soon
With peace lasting all night long.

White Supremacy

Segregationists
Extolling white privilege
American blight

White supremacy
Brash, bigoted, brazen breed
Hidden racism

Problematic

Disillusionment
Nothing new under the sun
The soul bears witness

When we two parted
Sweetness on the desert air
Such guilty pleasures

Little Miss Muppet
Supplying chilled curds and whey
A woman of means

Chagrined

The edge of madness
Other side of paradise
A heart of darkness

Lie down in darkness
The other side of midnight
A call to be wild

A world of strangers
A clear and present danger
A separate peace

Second Thoughts

The sound of fury
With rue the heart is laden
Pending disaster

Pessimistic

Cornered, cringing, clinging to
       false hope
Overcome with fear and trembling
Waiting and watching warily
Agonizing about the unknown
Awaiting the worst outcome
Reluctant to act, reeling from alarm,
       ravaged with dread
Danger impending; distressed by defeat
Shrinking, shivering, shackled by doubt
Frozen in fear

Worth Considering

Things are as they are
A time of indifference
Being and nothing

The edge of sadness
The world is too much with us
The turn of the screw

Great expectations
An elephant in the room
Dissatisfaction

Trying Times

Invasive species
Yellow-legged hornets
Hurting honeybees

Trying times take toll
Devastating drought distend
Flagrant forest fires

Pestilence persists
Wailings and gnashing of teeth
End-times eminent

In the Garden

Rib taken from Adam
Mother of all who have life
Tempted by Satan

Ate forbidden fruit
Knowledge of good and evil
Banished from Eden

The judgement of God
Lifetime pain…labor 'til death
The weight of the world

Heart Throbs

Do you think of me
As I think of you
Often and with fondness
Amid skies of blue?

I would like to know
And not sit and stew
From my vantage point
You haven't a clue.

My heart pines away
As my curiosity grew
My body tingles
With feelings for you.

With you on my mind
The dark days are few
Memories of your touch
Make me feel brand new.

Heartbreak

Heartbreak is real…
        ominous…tangible…crushing…
        shattering…wrenching…
        mournful…
Emotions teem with disappointment
Awash with ache within every fiber
        and essence of being
Reeling recollections rampant…
        racked with remorse
        pining in sorrow
Thrashed with longing…
    torn with regret
Tears of release…
    cleansing…healing…
Time to move on.

Unhinged

Shivering in fear, shaken with terror
Cold chills creeping through my being
Anxiously anticipating disaster
Racing heartbeat, raging thoughts
Erratic behavior
Distraught…
Dazed…
Confused…
Unhinged

Fantasyland

Fanciful notions dancing through the mind
Amazing feelings of rapture
No thoughts of gloom and doom
Taming the dreadful dragons
Airy images of reality
Surreal visions in a trip to happy-land
Yielding to the land of dreams…

Teeming with Life

*Great things are not done by impulse but by a series of
small things brought together.*

Van Gogh

Flesh Peddlers

Pimps procuring prostitutes
Alluring ladies of the evening peddling flesh
Seductresses barely clad in skimpy dress
Promenading the blue-light district
Hawking their fleshy charms
Luring their cruising customers:
Frustrated lovers
Forlorn husbands
Deviant devils
Closet voyeurs
Secretive sadists
Curious youth
Pernicious predators
Potential prospects…
Nameless Johns trolling during the wee hours
Hunting for a willing vamp
    To ply her trade
    To broker a deal
    To turn a trick
    To pay a bill
    To stoke an ego
    To scratch an itch

To quench a thirst…
To forget for a time
To lose oneself for a moment
Lost in Lethe's allure.

Cult Following

Dazzled by celebrity allure
Impressed by sylvan tongue and glib speech
Claims of wealth and splendor
Theatrical display of grandeur
Avid converts cling in adoration
To the Teflon Don of politics
Often posturing before cameras
Ranting misinformation and weaving a web of lies
Rallying an angry MAGA mob

Human Cargo

Fetched from across expansive danger waters
Launched from the Gulf of Guinea in Africa
Enslaved ebon bodies bound in chains
Shipped on a bill-of-laden to the Americas.
Heaped from stem to stern in the bowels of cargo ships
Precarious voyage on perilous high seas
Ending at foreign ports of the West Indies and the
       American continents
Darkling daughters and sons, parents and children
       wrenched apart, breaking bonds, dispersing families,
       stifling customs, forbidding flight...
Dealt with as chattel, mere nameless beasts of burden
       led to the auction block:
Extracted...exploited...exhibited...examined...
Restrained resources: fresh flesh rendered at an open market
Sold to the highest bidder

Silence

Terrapin toddling along the by-way
Utterly oblivious to the world around him
Ready to retreat into a shell
Tucked away from fear, hurt, or danger
Like countless passive citizens
      sitting in silence
Eschewing right for wrong…

Rampage

Renegade raging…
Running for cover:
screaming…ducking…dodging…falling…
Another crazed gunman on a tear
Mowing down innocent victims:

> Mothers, fathers
> Sons, daughters
> Brothers, sisters
> Strangers, friends…

Persons going about the day's affairs; in the right place,
> at the wrong time
Anticipating an uneventful, routine day
Getting alarmed by the sound of gunfire
Ending expectations for hundreds of grieving families

Food for Thought

Honeysuckle
Honeysuckle
Savory, sweet
Bestowing bees
A tasty treat

Honeysuckle
Honeysuckle
Showy flowers neat
Holding hummingbirds
A ration replete

Honeysuckle
Honeysuckle
Verdant vine
Wandering wildly
No matter the kind.

Snowy Owl

Captivating bird
Ghostly Arctic predator
Surviving the cold

Massive yellow eyes
Opportunistic hunter
Radar-like hearing

Whitecoat camouflage
With thick plumage protection
Conserves body heat

Barking—not hooting
Marking its territory
Dive-bombing defense

Showy snowy owl
Of silent-flight fringed feathers
Striking bird of prey

Prowling Tiger

Tawny striped feline on the prowl
Imposing jungle predator, slinking
    through the undergrowth on silent padded
    paws
Gazing with precision…
    gauging the distance
Every sense alert, eying possible prey
Stealthy savage hunter ready to pounce
Successful snare slaughtered
Sinewy fleshy meal
Spoils of victory

Water Wizards

Canny camouflage
Magical sea denizens
The perfect disguise

Leafy sea dragon
Lodging among the seaweed
Hiding in plain sight

Buoyant cuttlefish
Magical quick-change artist
Slick water wizard

Sit-and-wait stonefish
Blending with environment
Master of disguise

Bear Bustle

Big burly furry beast, browsing its territory
Engorging in season berries…nuts…
Fish…insects…honey…
Anticipating a long cold winter
Readying for hibernation

Blowfly

Fearless foul insect, droning in flight
Alighting on decaying matter or untended food
Yielding plaints and peril…

Crafty Crows

Clever creative glossy black bird,
Capable of solving complex problems
Recognizing potential threats,
Remembering grievances
Holding grudges
Opportunistic feeder, from crops to carrion
Warning wayfarers with a caw call of caution
Smart-aleck animal.

Fearless Hunter

Secretary bird
Clad in britches and tailcoat
Land-roving raptor

Quill-like feathered crest
Fleet-footed avian fowl
Archer of serpents

Showy Toucan

Celebrated bird
Brightly marked colorful feathers
Large, oversized bill

Strong short legs, small wings
Passerine bird family
Rounded tail, thick neck

Vocal social bird
Curious, inquisitive
Boisterous beaked brood

Giant Redwood

A living giant
Magnificent redwood tree
Pioneer species

Coniferous tree
Long evergreen awl-shaped leaves
With spirally shoots

Columnar trunk
Adaptative to forest fires
Long-lasting lineage

Enduring redwood
Fibrous, spongy red-orange bark
Ancient survivor

Tuckaleechee Caverns

Mystical marvel
At Tuckaleechee Caverns
A peaceful valley

Ancient formations
Scenic natural wonder
Breathtaking beauty

Underground structures
Stalagmites and stalactites
Nature at its best

Linville Caverns

Inside a mountain
Hidden world's wondrous splendor
Shady dolomite

Natural wonder
Fantastic festoons of rock
Fine earthy pendants

Surging stream scours through
An active limestone cavern
With bottomless pool

Rocky Mountain Goat

Rocky mountain goat
A cloven-hoofed animal
Sure-footed climber

Bearded bob-tailed beast
Woolly gray-white double coat
Withstanding the cold

On sheer rock faces
At extreme elevations
Near-vertical cliffs

Powerful shoulders
Sturdy body, short stout legs
Hazarding the heights

Noisy Takahe

Noisy takahe
Blue and green silky plumage
A flightless swamphen

Short crayfish red legs
Dark blue head with massive beak
Scarlet frontal shield

Stocky…powerful
Member of rail family
Edge of extinction

Fetid Feast

Buzzards big as turkeys
Flopping on the highway
Drawn to the fetid smell of decaying flesh
Feasting on carrion
Easy pickings of day-old roadkill
Tasty meal for nature's clean-up crew.

Wandering Within Wonderland

Wherever you go, go with all your heart.

Confucius

Old Glory

On windy days unfurled, flapping in the breeze,
      Undulating on the air currents
Lashed to a sturdy metal pole
Dressed in red and white colonial stripes
Graced with a patch of royal blue,
      Lightly sprinkled with fifty stately stars
Often hanging loosely on calm, listless days,
      As if weary from the tumult of the times
Ready to…
      Stand up for democracy
      Fight for freedom
      Lead the charge in battle
      Champion victory
      Even drape the bier of fallen patriots
Yet welcome foreigners seeking refuge…

Genteel Gent

Genteel giant; no glib tongue
Every woman's dreamboat
Not nasty nor mean-spirited
No gossipmonger
Touch of class
Liquid voice speaking languid words
Engaging repartee, encouraging words of solace
Man of means
Arresting gaze
Art of persuasion…
Next conquest?

Walking in the Newness of Life

Reared with a righteous upbringing
Robust youth playing sports
Later frequenting the Harlem District in the city,
        straying from pious roots
            Neglecting to tread the path of righteousness,
            nearly escaping several brushes with death,
            serving a stint behind bars
Now, touched by the Holy Spirit,
        A new creation emerges…

I become aware that my life has been spared
        to fulfill a divine purpose,
Eagerly walking in the newness of life…

Love or Lust?

Racing pulse at the mere thought of you
Object of my desire
Nearly out of my mind
Needing to hold you close
Is this yearning love or lust?
Emotional upheaval
Near the breaking point, eaten up with longing
Even thought of making the first move,
       letting you know my feelings,
       giving you my number
Loss of nerve prevails
Settled for a chance meeting,
       an occasional glimpse
Our stars have not aligned

Now or never?
Nothing ventured…nothing gained…

Entranced

The mere thought of you
Takes my breath away
But you seem to be walking
On feet made of clay…

I look at you with longing
Imploring you with my eyes
(Thankful you can't read my mind
You'd be quite surprised…)

Day by day, I count the hours
When I next will see you again
Not even a mere hug in greeting
Can tamp the fire raging within…

It seems as if I must settle
For us to warp and wend
Maybe one day you'll realize
I want to be more than friends.

Wretchedness

I packed my heart aggrieved
To harden in the deep freeze
There it sets in the dark
Protected from the spark
Of flame in your eyes
No longer a prize
As it was from the start
To melt with such ease.

Christmas *Ad Nauseam*

The world is filled with the joy of Christmas:
> Sleighbells ringing
> Merchants vending
> Carolers singing
> Shoppers spending
> Cash registers chinging…

The world is thrilled with the wonder of Christmas:
> Parents rushing
> Santa believed
> Children gushing
> Presents received
> Debts crushing…

The world has parlayed
The thrust of Christmas
The birth of the Holy Babe
The Heir we can trust.

In the Mix

It came upon a midnight clear
One silent, holy night
A star in Bethlehem appeared
To guide us to the Light.

Joy to the world—the first Noel
The herald angels sing
O come, o come Immanuel
Glory to the Newborn King.

Joy to the World

Joy to the world, a child is born
Glory to God, a son is given
During this festive holiday season
Extol the Anointed Babe from heaven.

All heaven and nature sing
The wondrous virgin birth
Beloved Son, Heir of all things
Hail the greatest gift of worth.

Gift of God, the Prince of Peace
Bread of Life, Great High Priest
King of Kings, a carpenter's son
Word of God, Holy and Just One,
Blessed Messiah, Light Eternal,
O Lamb of God—Immanuel.

A Gift at Christmastime

Something special: being alive still,
Experiencing the so-called golden years,
Not yet being considered over-the-hill
Experiencing aging without fear.

Through the years gaining wisdom,
No longer rushing here and there,
Doing as much as can be done
To tame those glaring gray hairs.

Enjoying life to the best of my ability,
Grateful not to be sinking into senility,
Counting my blessings one by one,
As I approach the setting of the sun:
      Pleased to be breathing
        Lucky to have loved ones
            to comfort or console
Happy for the gift of laughter
Blessed not to stress about
      the small stuff
Fortunate to do what I please
      when I want to

Grateful for the family I've had
	and the feelings we've shared
Appreciative of my experiences
	and the lessons they taught me
Simply content just to be moseying along
My what a gracious present:
To be granted longevity: the gift of life

Festive Feeling

Frosty the Snowman and fake Santa Clauses
Eating gingerbread cookies and enjoying eggnog
Singing carols of comfort and joy
Tidings of merriment and happiness
In homes, towns, neighborhoods, shopping malls…
Various light and decorative displays
Eclipsing the birth of the blessed Savior of mankind.

Frosty Morning

Frigid air…
Frosty rooftops…
Icicles hanging…
Frozen landscape…

Reaching for a furry coat and fuzzy gloves
Record low temperature
      Old record broken
      Out-and-out icy cold
Slipping on a slippery walkway
Testing my agility and equilibrium
Yearning for summer's warmth

Amazon Rainforest

Amazon Basin
No substantial dry season
Moist broadleaf region

Closed tree canopy
Marks moisture-dependent growth
Amazon jungle

High humidity
Moist layer of leaf litter
Tropical forest

Absence of wildfires
Diverse flora and fauna
Treasure of nature

Land of Extremes

Desolate landscape…devil's golf course
Extreme environment…edge of the world…
      Solar radiation
      Searing daytime heat
      Stinging cold nights
      Scant precipitation
      Sparse vegetation
      Sterile salt flats
      Spasmatic sand dunes
      Serrated soil
Extreme weather patterns
Rain-shuttered expanse
Death Valley Desert
Rugged beauty
Test of endurance

Touch and Go

Tearing down the highway
Racing past vehicles in the right lane
Artfully dodging the blue-lighted highway patrol
Absence of fear
Vowing to stay vigilant.
Eating up the miles at top speed
Lead-foot driver with nothing to lose.

Solar Conversion

Skies of blue and solar panels galore
Over stretches of farm fields
Following the sun
Latched low to the earth
Acre after acre
Row after row
As orderly as a fruit orchard
Reaping tons of amperes
Renewable energy resource
Pivotal power

Rejection

Rueful regrets resonate
Ego-deflating evidence of refusal
Just a shrug of indifference
>Jeopardizing friendship...
>harmony...
>stasis...
Edge of sadness
Complete disappointment...
>Cold shoulder dismissal...
Cold water on passion's flame
Total eclipse of the heart
In the dumps
>If only...
On-set of distress
Nothing encouraging...
Not a sliver of hope

Farther on Down the Road, a volume of assorted poetic forms and themes and purposes with a hint of folk wisdom, expresses sentiments about life's pathway for those journeying farther on down the road. The four sections contain tersely formed verses of reflections of the soul and observations about nature's splendor ranging from the whimsical to witty, from the weird to wanton, from the wild to wrenching, from the wise to moribund.